OPTIONS TRADING

Basics Explained:

Understanding the Concepts of Options

BORIS TIMM

[:Copyright:] © 2019 by Boris Timm

All rights reserved. No part of this publication may be reproduced, distributed, or transmitted in any form or by any means, including photocopying, recording, or other electronic or mechanical methods, without the prior written permission of the publisher, except in the case of brief quotations embodied in critical reviews and certain other noncommercial uses permitted by copyright law.

Although every precaution has been taken to verify the accuracy of the information contained herein, the author and publisher assume no responsibility for any errors or omissions. No liability is assumed for damages that may result from the use of information contained within.

Table of Contents

Introduction 1

Chapter 1: Option Trading Basics 5

Chapter 2: Trading Fundamentals 11
    Options Trading: What You Must Know 16

Chapter 3: Understanding the Risks in Option Trading 21

Chapter 4: Message to the Novices in Option Trading 39

Chapter 5: Option Trading Advice 53
    Option Trading Terminologies: Must-Know 58

Chapter 6: Why Size Matters - Especially in Options Trading 65

Chapter 7: Using Option Greeks in Option Trading 81

Chapter 8: Options Trading Strategies - Commodity, Currency Spread and Carry Trading 85
    Option Trading Strategies For Long Term Investors ... 90
    Why Use Option Trading Strategies? 96
    The Best Option Trading Software 101

Chapter 9: Trading Options Like the Pros 107

Conclusion 111

Introduction

Thousands of small retail traders are making a living, and some a fortune, from trading options and you are eager to take a shot at it too, aren't you? So, what are some of the things you must know in order to master options trading?

In my previous eBook "A Simple Guide to Investing in Turnaround Stocks - How to Successfully Invest in Stocks of Turnaround Companies" I mentioned some of the benefits of investing in stocks as high return on investment and diversification. However option trading is in the same line.

The options market is very complex. Trading options without a system is like building a house without a blueprint. Volatility, time and stock movement can all affect your profitability. You need to be cognizant of each of these variables. It is easy to be swayed by emotion when the market is moving.

Having a system helps to control your reaction to those very natural and normal emotions. How often have you sat and watched a trade lose money the instant your buy order filled? Or, have you ever watched a stock skyrocket in price while you are pondering over whether or not to buy it?

Having a structured plan in place is crucial to make sound and objective trading decisions. By creating and following a good system, you can hone your trading executions to be as emotionless and automatic as a computer.

In this eBook I will take you through the nitty gritty of Options trading in general. Knowledge is power, the power to know HOW and WHEN to make decisions in Options Trading is the key to top class profits.

Tarry along!!!

CHAPTER 1

Option Trading Basics

If you are into trading, you will surely know about options trading. Most people assume that they know all the terms related to trading options and go ahead with their trading methods.

Online trading has made tremendous advancement and you need to keep abreast of all the new happenings. You will also have to check out the forex options when you are doing online trading.

A highly successful financial product nowadays, stock options offer the investor flexibility, diversification and control to protect his/her stock portfolio or generate more investment income. Options are advantageous because they can be used under almost every market condition and for almost every investment objective.

Options also help the investor to purchase stock at a lower price and to benefit from a stock price's rise or fall without owing the stock or selling it outright.

As options have a unique risk/reward structure, they can be used in combination with other option contracts and/or other financial tools to seek profits or protection.

Using stock options, investors can fix the price for a specific period of time, at which an investor can buy or dispose of 100 shares of stock for a premium that is only a percentage of what one would pay to own the stock outright. This helps investors to leverage their investment power while increasing their potential reward from a stock's price fluctuations.

As far as stock options are concerned, there are only limited risks for buyers. In no way can an option buyer lose more than the price of the option, the premium. With the right to purchase or sell the underlying security at a specific price expiring on a given date, the option will expire worthless if the conditions for profitable exercise or sale of the contract are not met by the expiry date.

Even as options offer many investment benefits, they are not meant for everyone. Just as one's returns can be large, so too can the losses – leverage. Moreover, the means for realizing the potential for financial success in option trading may be difficult to create or identify.

A large amount of information must be processed before an informed trading decision can be arrived at. Option trading is more complicated than stock trading because traders must choose from many variables besides the direction they believe the market will move.

Careful consideration and sound money management techniques are a must for successful option trading.

The meaning of an option has many connotations and you need to understand this word only too well when doing the online trading. An option is financial instrument that is derived from the price of the underlying instrument.

An option is of two types. The first type is the call option and the second is the put option. Understanding the call and put options is quite important to gain expertise in online trading. When looking at the trading options, you will also have to manage your finances properly and invest wisely.

It is also very important to know the different ways of how to trade options in the current market scenario. If you want to make the maximum advantage of the volatility in the commodities market, you will have to try out the FCD trading.

The key terms that you need to understand when you are doing online trading are Commodities Trading, Trading Commodities, Trading Metals, Options CFDs, stock indices, Stock Index CFDs, Index Trading, Stock Index Trading, CFD Trading, CFD Provider, and CFDs.

The best way to get some information on these terms is by searching them on the Internet. If you are getting totally confused, it makes more sense to check out with someone who knows these terms properly. You may have to spend at least a week in understanding these terms.

Once you are comfortable with these terms, you will have to get into the procedures for trading. Currently, trading gold may seem to be very good and profitable, but there are many other options that would also give you an equally good return.

In all stock market trading deals, it is seen that people do the buying and selling without actually understanding the basic guidelines.

If you are interested in CFD trading or contract for difference trading, you will have to first understand the basics of CFDs, the process of trading CFDs, and identify the risks that are involved during contract for difference trading.

Contract for difference trading is best understood when an example is taken. So, find out a website that will give you the examples. After you have got a website that gives you all the best examples, you will have to move on and check out the process of contract for difference trading. When seeing the examples, you may be treated to several numbers and calculations.

Such calculations are inevitable and you have to bear with it. Generally with a little practice and good basics, you will have a clearer understanding of the procedures and concepts of contract for difference trading. Selecting the best website for your options trading is very important. So, make sure that you get a good website for all your trading requirements.

CHAPTER 2

Trading Fundamentals

Succeeding with options is not always the easiest thing to achieve. Sure, there are some that have made a great success in their ventures into the world of options trading. These people are among those that many will look towards as inspiration for their options trading adventures.

Then, there will be those that will look towards these success stories for more than inspiration. They will look towards successful options traders as those to duplicate. Or, more accurately, they will try to duplicate the trading methods and strategies of the trader.

While it is certainly a wise thing to look towards the trading methods of a successful trader, duplicating the steps of the trader alone may not prove to be the best strategy. The reason for this is that there are other factors that go into the process of developing a trading strategy than just the execution of the trades.

Personal factors will go into the development of a methodology. In some instances, there will be psychological factors that will be developed into the trading plans. Understanding such components is vital to exploring a trading method to make sure it is valuable to your goals.

Actually, it would not hurt to explore your own psychological factors and facets prior to looking seriously at trading. Now, some may assume such assessments are little more than 'psycho-babble' that seek to examine options trading from an over-analytical perspective.

This may be the case in some instances but as a general explanation of what motivates people towards options trading, it is definitely not something you want to overlook. By having a clear understanding of your own psychological makeup, you can develop the proper insight into how to be effective in the art of trading.

Simply put, some people are more cut out for options trading than others. Those that are conservative in their investment strategies might wish to limit options trading to a smaller part of their overall portfolio.

Those that can be considered quite aggressive in their approach may look towards possibly using options as a hedge to their portfolio. Again, your own personal psychological makeup regarding comfort levels of trading in essential in options. This will certainly help promote your ability to discover the proper answer to whether or not you are cut out for options trading.

How can you discover whether or not you have the mindset of an options trader? The first step involves honestly answering whether or not you are someone that possesses the discipline to be an options trader. Some may believe they have the discipline to succeed.

However, believing you possess certain attributes to a specific degree and actually possessing those attributes to the proper degree are two completely different things. Knowing exactly where you stand in terms of your mindset and your levels of discipline will aid in boosting your chances of success.

For example, someone who needs to keep fiddling with their account by buying and selling every few days isn't someone who should be investing in options! The commissions alone will eat you up. Similarly someone who like a lot of excitement in their trading should probably stay away from options.

Having a quality options trading strategy is helpful. Putting the options trading strategy through to fruition is even more helpful. But, once again, there is a big difference in having the desire to follow such a process and actually following through with it.

Those that are able to follow through with such steps may be limited in number. No, that is not said as a means of undermining anyone's motivation, morale, or desire. Rather, it is meant as a way of properly forecasting the management of your venture and assessing the risk of getting involved with options trading. You also need a plan for when the market goes against your strategy, so that you don't make decisions because you're panicking.

Yes, trading in options needs to be looked from the perspective of managing a small business. When operating a small business, you need to assess the risk associated with a venture. You also need to assess the risks and potentials associated with the success or failure of the business.

This same ideology needs to be put towards options trading. If you can honestly assess yourself as someone with the self discipline to follow through with a reliable options trading strategy, then you may very well be extremely successful with options trading.

Also, how well can you handle losing trades? Are you able to handle losses and pick things up and start the process over again? If you are then you may very well embody the proper psychological makeup for succeeding with options trading. Those that cannot handle the pressure of the occasional loss would be better served looking towards another investing strategy.

Options Trading: What You Must Know

Stock options are derivatives of shares. This means that you need to know what shares are in the first place in order to understand the role of options and how options work. In fact, you will need to be a master of stock and shares behavior before you could be a master of options trading because options are merely tools that help you exploit these stock and shares behavior profitably.

Sounds like common sense but most options traders start out thinking options are just "another stock" which you simply buy low and sell high.

Those who jump into their first options trade like this usually get a shock of their lives when they either realize that options don't quite move the way they expect them to move and don't quite behave the way they expect them to behave. Knowing how options work and what their underlying mechanisms are, the logic behind call and put options are the basic knowledge all master options traders need.

The real magic of options trading lies not in simply buying call options for stocks expected to go up or buying put options for stocks expected to go down. The real magic of options trading lie in the universe of options strategies which allows you to profit not only from an upwards or downwards market but even in a neutral or volatile one.

You probably won't be able to learn, practice and master each and every of the hundreds of options strategies but you should have at least one or two options strategies of each class that you are totally familiar with and have paper traded so that you have a weapon for each market condition.

Technical Analysis

Technical analysis is particularly important for options trading as it is through technical analysis that you can make trend analysis in order to know what class of options strategy to apply in the first place.

Technical analysis is extremely important in options trading also due to the fact that entry and exit timing is extremely important in options trading where there is a fixed expiration. Technical analysis has been used over the decades as a tool for precision entry and exit and is now an important tool in options trading.

In reference to my eBOOK, "A Simple Guide to Investing in Turnaround Stocks how to successfully invest in Stocks of Turnaround Companies" Technical analysis software's can help a trader in exploiting the BSE and NSE for their diverse day trading and investment opportunities.

These can be charting modules which align to methods of technical analysis and stock analysis. The software also helps in drafting the candlestick patterns.

Options Greeks

Options Greeks are the mathematical components that define how a particular option would behave in response to factors such as changes in the price of the underlying stock, changes in volatility, changes in interest rate and time decay. An intimate understanding of all the options Greeks allows you to better understand and predict the behavior of an options position. It also allows you to make intricate adjustments to your options position in order to create a payoff profile that conforms to the exact predicted behavior of the price of the underlying asset.

Delta Neutral Trading

Delta neutral trading is the ability to tweak a position's delta status to a level that is zero or almost zero such that small volatilities in the price of the underlying asset do not affect the value of the overall position. When delta neutral trading is performed correctly, it could even be used as a hedge which profits no matter which direction the price of the underlying asset breaks out into next. This can only be achieved by a combination of call options, put options, the underlying asset and even futures. Different situations require a different approach to delta neutral hedging and that is why it takes a strong knowledge in all of these instruments in order to do delta neutral trading well.

Mastering all of the above will allow you to realize your dream as a master options trader and be able to make a living off trading options. Are you able to master all of the above?

CHAPTER 3

Understanding the Risks in Option Trading

You must have heard horror stories surrounding options trading before. Stories such as how some people lose their whole account within a few days and even stories of options traders going bankrupt in express time.

These stories have no doubt cast a shadow over options trading and there are even people who now tout that options trading is as risky as futures trading.

Well, strange thing is, after more than 15 years of trading options, I have never experienced losing all my money within a few days nor going bankrupt. This led me to wonder why these things happen to some options traders.

After some investigation, I conclude that it is not options trading that breaks accounts but specific things some options traders tend to do, especially beginners, that opens the door to such financial disasters. I narrowed these reasons down to two main ones.

The first of these is that some options traders trade options just like they trade stocks; buying call options with their whole account on that one "hot stock."

Yes, this is the number reason why most options beginners lose their shirt. Most beginners to options trading do with call options exactly what they do with stocks when they have a "hot tip"; throwing their whole account into that single "hot" trade.

Now, this isn't that big a problem in stock trading because if the stock didn't move as expected, the trader could simply continue to hold the position until it does, sometimes for years.

However, when you buy call options on stocks that didn't eventually move up as expected, the call options can expire worthless by expiration, taking your WHOLE account with it if you bought those call options with all the money you had!

This problem is made even more pronounced by the fact that options have a definite expiration date that goes from a few months to a year for some stocks but never forever. This means that you do not have the luxury of holding on to bad trades forever, hoping they will come back in a few years time.

Professional options traders like me only enter a single position with money we can afford to lose. If I intend to lose no more than 10% of my account on any one trade, I do not use more than 10% of my account in a single trade.

That's right, you NEVER buy a single options position or options contract with all the money you have! Although that would have made sense in stock trading, it is pure suicide and gamble in options trading.

The other reason is trading credit spreads or naked option writing without using stop loss.

Many options beginners were taken in by the apparent "free money" phenomena of writing naked options positions unaware that most of these credit strategies have unlimited loss potential.

For instance, if you wrote call options (shorting call options), you would make a fixed premium in profit if the stock went downwards or sideways. Some "gurus" call this "playing bookmaker".

Well, they are right that you are playing bookmaker to gamblers by selling options to them but they forgot to mention the fact that sometimes, gamblers win big too.

OPTIONS TRADING

When you write call options, your position will make an incrementally bigger loss as the stock price rises!

It will continue to make bigger and bigger loss as long as the stock continues to rise. This is what is known as an unlimited loss position. This loss is often, or always, much bigger than the premium you received from selling the options.

Before you know it, your entire account is wiped out on this one trade because the stock refused to go down as you expected it to.

Does that mean we should not trade credit spreads or naked writes ever again? Not really. These are excellent options strategies but only if you trade them using a specific and definite stop loss point.

Yes, most options trading beginners trade such unlimited loss potential credit spreads with stop loss points but most of them give in to emotion when it's time to stop loss and hold their positions beyond their stop loss points in hope that things will turn around, which most often, they never do.

Professional options traders always trade unlimited loss potential positions with an AUTOMATED stop loss point. That's right, automated stop loss that works without human involvement. This can be in the form of a stop limit, contingent order or trailing stop loss order.

As long as you do not have to physically execute the stop loss. Physically executed stop losses are stop losses that rarely gets executed. Remember that.

Buying options with your whole account and trading unlimited loss potential options positions without stop loss points are the two main reasons most options beginners lose their shirt. Take heed of my advice here and you would go through your initial options trading years in much more safety.

Online trading sites are now providing the opportunity for all investors to pursue option trading in the stock market. There is a broad range of availability, but an individual should understand the difference between the existing types prior to choosing this type of investment. There are three main options available; puts, calls and warrants.

Option trading has become available through a wide array of online investment sites. Using a retirement or investment account, a person now has the capabilities to trade these types of securities.

There are several different types of options available to the consumer such as puts, calls and warrants. In order to trade these devices on the stock market, it is important to understand what they are.

A contract that states the seller of an asset will agree to do so at a stated price on a certain date is what is known as a put. This type of contract is created by an individual and then purchased by another at a fee, after which it is traded on the stock market.

People buy the contracts, gambling on the directional movement of the price of the good. The final purchaser hopes it will increase, so they can buy for less than market value.

When a person purchases a call, they anticipate that the price of the underlying asset will fall. This is because a call is an option to sell a good or security. They will then collect more than the worth of the underlying items.

A warrant is slightly different in that it is usually issued by a company allowing the contract holder to purchase a security at a given price for a set period of time. So, during that time frame, if the market price of the security increases, the owner can buy the stock and sell it immediately for a profit.

It is not required that the underlying asset be purchased by the buyer. The buyer is the person holding the contract and that has the right to purchase the items if they choose to. The seller, maker, or writer, as the contract creator is called, must sell or buy the asset if the buyer elects to use the terms that were set forth.

To trade these types of contracts is very similar to that of regular stocks or mutual funds. The risk associated with options is great because the investor must accurately guess price movements. However, due to use of leverage, it can be a very profitable means of trading as well with enormous potential for gain. In fact, puts have unlimited gain potential.

Listed on the Philadelphia, CBOE, Pacific and AMEX stock exchanges, most online investment institution now grant individual investors the opportunity to trade options. They must state their interest and claim to have the appropriate knowledge first, however.

Placing them on an exchange enabled expiration dates to be standardized so that they are on the third Friday of the month.

There are numerous types of assets for which options are written. These include exchanges, stock indexes, debt securities, and currencies. The buyer is then making a call as to whether the price of each of these is going to move in a certain direction based upon whether a put or call has been bought.

An investor stands to realize a good amount of gain potential, if they can also handle the risk associated with potential loss in option trading. By making it available through brokerage accounts of online banking institutions, many people now have accessFree Reprint Articles, but they must first understand how to use it.

Furthermore, Option traders often complain about their inability to learn the ropes of stock options trading and hence fail to create as much capital as they want to.

The most important element that a trader should keep in mind is the existence of various risks associated with stock options trading and the ways to deal with them, according to one's capabilities.

Knowing about the relevant risks would allow the traders to beware of them from beforehand while investing a large amount of money.

As a matter of fact, trading with stock options is not for the faint-hearted traders as it expects one to be able to bear and confront risks and loss. It is definitely not all about winning and gains, one must learn to loose and face defeat, to gain expertise and insight about this field.

If this field ensures gains in a blink of an eye, it can also take the entire profit away within a drop of a hat. Hence, one needs to prepare himself to face both profits and losses. A trader is thus often found to modify, re-assess and review his trading strategy according to the latest and relevant market scenario, price movements and other financial indicators, to avoid risks of loss.

Before starting off in stock options, a trader should know the difference between investing and options trading. The later is considered to be a kind of speculation wherein the trader take upon a business risk with a hope of gaining profit out of market and price fluctuations of stocks. Certain skills like prediction of trading outcomes, analyzing market trends and swings, assessing the price movements and understanding the indicators, are necessary to make a considerable amount of profit as well as to manage and deal with risks and volatility.

In options trading, it is more important to know about the probable risk factors and loss-limits than to know about the profit-making possibilities. Knowing about the upcoming risk factor would immunize the trader about the losses and would also give him time to prepare against it.

Traders mostly prefer to keep themselves updated with the latest information, data-feed, market and price movements of stocks and shares, in order to make a correct prediction and to avoid risks. However, a trader should always analyze his individual risk-bearing abilities and trading style in order to set up a realistic financial goal out of options trading.

Last but not the least, the traders should also gain expertise and insight about reading and comprehending the market signals depicted by system indicators which can be fixed with the trader's computer system, displayed in the form of charts, filters, price fluctuations etc.

For a trader it is always advisable to avoid any risk situation and that can be done to a large extent by sticking to the trading strategy or the system with patience and perseverance.

Risks can also be avoided by staying away from insensible trading actions out of emotional pressures and external influences. The most suggested way is to first start with paper-trading in order to learn the art and the rules without any money losses.

With any business venture there are always risks - and the risks of options trading are no different. Understanding these risks is crucial to successful trading.

In fact, launching boldly into the world of options trading without knowing what you're up against, is like a business without a strategy or sense of direction.

If you want to make a regular income from trading you have to approach it with the mindset of a businessperson. You have to do your SWOT analysis - strengths, weaknesses, opportunities and threats. This article is primarily about the "weaknesses and threats" aspect.

Enemy Number One - Time Decay

Options are unlike any other derivative financial instrument in that their value decays with the passing of time. During the final 30 days of an options life, its value decays at a much faster and more exponential rate than in all its previous life.

You need to be aware of this, the most notorious of all the risks of options trading, and use it to your advantage when implementing your option trading strategies.

If you know who your enemy is, you can not only avoid the dangers of approaching it the wrong way, but in the world of stock market trading, you can also turn this enemy into your best friend.

One of the great advantages of options trading is that you can not only BUY option contracts, but also create new ones out of nothing and SELL them to the market. We call the 'buying' end 'going long' while the 'selling end' is 'going short'. Most of the risks of options trading fall into the lap of those who 'go long' options, due to the disease of time decay.

If you buy options in the hope of selling for a profit, you need to feel sure that the underlying stock, commodity of whatever, will move to your desired target reasonably quickly, otherwise time decay will eat into your profits.

There are ways to minimise this, such as buying "deep-in-the-money" options, where most of their value is "intrinsic value" and less "time value". Another alternative is to purchase long-dated options, i.e. with an expiry date at least 90 days away.

This will give you more time to be right and provided they are 'in-the-money' will be less affected by time decay.

Your Enemy Becomes Your Friend

So how can you use time decay to your advantage and minimise the risks of options trading? We have already mentioned that you can SELL (go short) options contracts as well as buy them. This allows the trader to construct combinations of long and short positions in a way that use time decay to your advantage. It is well known that on average, 85 percent of options contracts expire worthless.

So that means that if you're on the selling end of the deal, your average risk is reduced from 85 percent to the remaining 15 percent who have sold those contracts.

There are a number of option trading strategies which allow you to do this, such as credit spreads, butterfly spreads, iron condors, ratio spreads and covered calls. There are many ways you can use 'short' options to reduce the risks of options trading.

Non-directional Trading

Another risk, which is not limited to option trading, is the need to be able to predict the future direction of the underlying market in order to profit.

But did you know that there are option trading strategies such as the straddle or options strangle, which allow you to effectively take a bet both ways. You don't care which way the market moves, as long as it goes somewhere within a short space of time.

The run-up to an upcoming earnings report is one of the best times to implement this strategy, as markets are anticipating the impending news.

Range Trading Strategies

Since time decay is "enemy number one" among the risks of options trading, it is at its worst when market price action is going nowhere. Sideways trending markets can kill an option's value very quickly.

But if you're on the selling end of such a contract, it is where you make your profit. There are a number of option range trading strategies you can take advantage of.

The risks of options trading need not be feared if you know how to handle them. Options are very flexible in that positions, once entered, can also be adjusted as you see market price movements taking shape. Even losing positions can be turned into winning ones.

CHAPTER 4

Message to the Novices in Option Trading

For anybody who may be only a beginner in option trading and just beginning your learning journey, we have a few valuable tips here for you. If you take them seriously, they might mean the difference between significant and consistent income and wiping out your entire trading bank.

What I'm going to explain to you, is from someone who has lost his hard earned money in days gone by - and I would like to share with you reasons why such things happen, in the hope you can avoid the same pitfalls.

The financial markets can be a truly rewarding friend if you treat them with respect, but when you believe you can outsmart them or pay no attention to what they are telling you, they can financially kill you. They are massive and there is more than enough room for everyone, nevertheless, you must be aware of the risks and be well prepared for them.

So, let us discuss the main things a newcomer to option trading should know.

You need to have the right frame of mind to tackle trading the markets. Since option trading is a heavily leveraged instrument, the astounding profits you are able to realize are offset by substantial losses should you choose to disregard it when things go wrong.

Things will always go wrong. You'll never get every trade correct. It's no different in any other type of traditional business - some transactions are profitable, others are not.

When you can look at it this way, that you are in a business (not just a part time hobby) and thus all transactions you undertake are in accordance with an overall business plan, there is a far better chance of succeeding.

Most businesses fail within the first year of operation, mainly because they don't plan carefully and know how they are going to use their financial resources to produce a profit. Your resources are your trading capital. You are buying and selling to make money. If you neglect your business (forget about your trades with the hope they might fix themselves) it's just like forgetting your customers and hoping they will serve themselves.

Experienced traders always say to the beginner in option trading, that 90 percent of trading success is all about psychology. The way you handle the decision to get into a trade and how you choose to get out are critical components for success.

Do you hesitate to "pull the trigger" when you see a positive setup, then regret it later when you see the spectacular results you missed out on? Do you find it difficult to accept that you have been wrong about a trade and cannot come to grips with taking a small loss?

You have to be capable of being honest with yourself about these things. Know yourself and what trading style you're better suited to. Are you a day-trader? Are you able to cope with the pressure? Maybe you are better off being a short term trader? Or if your life is otherwise busy, perhaps a longer term investment strategy might better suit your style?

Different Strokes for Different Folks

There are different trading styles you can utilize with option contracts. Some are high risk, high reward, and some low risk but lower returns. Do you need 50 percent yield on your trading bank each month, or would you be content with just 10 percent?

Whatever your response, how does that fit with the amount of capital you have to trade with and will that be enough for you to live on?

$100,000 on low risk positions bringing an average 5 to 15 percent per month is much easier and more manageable than $10,000 on high risk trades looking for a minimum 50 percent per month.

Educate Yourself

Maybe when getting started in option trading, you've read some books about technical analysis of stock charts and feel persuaded you'll be able to anticipate the short term direction of stocks. You've heard that with options you can make money whether the underlying is rising or falling - call options profit when it's rising and put options increase in value when the underlying is falling. Too easy!

But did you realize there are some much more advanced option trading strategies around, which allow you to make a good income from stocks on condition that they stay within certain price boundaries until expiration date but even if they don't, you can simply adjust your positions to make a profit anyway?

The Iron Condor is just one such strategy - two credit spreads facing opposite directions with a strike price difference in between. Beautiful for producing a profit within a $10 to $15 trading range over one to two months.

The learner in option trading is usually excited about future possibilities. I remember I was. You're going to be financially free, earning better than your old job. You've seen the light. You can sack your employer and work just one hour daily rather than toiling away for 40 hours a week. No doubt you've heard the "sell". Sounds so good doesn't it.

And indeed, the above can be true . . . IF you take it seriously, develop a passion for it, think of it as a business rather than a distraction, educate yourself properly and understand how and when to adapt each strategy to market conditions in a way that minimizes risk and maximizes profit.

Many option traders are earning a very healthy living. Others have rapidly eliminated their available funds so are very disillusioned. Like anything worthwhile, it doesn't come easily - but once it does, the rewards are worth it. If you are a beginner in option trading Health Fitness Articles, you have an interesting journey ahead.

Can Options Trading Turn You Into a Millionaire?

This is one of those questions I hear from people new to options trading all the time and not an easy question to answer in my opinion. Sure, options trading can create millionaires and many, including myself, have made more an a million trading options. However, can options trading turn YOU into a millionaire?

In a way, asking this question is as good as asking questions like:

Can trading stocks turn you into a millionaire?

Can trading futures turn you into a millionaire?

Can trading Forex turn you into a millionaire?

Can selling burgers turn you into a millionaire?

Can collecting coins turn you into a millionaire?

The answer to all of these questions is a resounding, YES.

The problem is, can YOU become a millionaire doing these things that have made OTHER people millionaires?

First of all, let's ascertain the theoretical possibility of making a million through options trading. Let's assume you have $5000 to start trading options with and you make an average of 50% per trade and compound your earnings. Here's your account status after a number of trades:

After first trade - $7500

Second - $11,250

Third - $16,875

Forth - $25,312.5

Fifth - $37,968.75

Eighth - $128,144.5

Fourteenth - $1,459,646

As you can see, it takes only 14 trades at 50% profit per trade, which is not a lot in options trading, to grow $5000 into a million. If you do only one of those trades per month, it takes you only slightly more than a year to become a millionaire.

As such, becoming a millionaire from options trading is clearly not outside the realm of possibility and clearly very fast if you do it right.

That leads us to the next question, are you able to produce a string of 14 straight wins at 50% per win? There is clearly no easy answer to this as well. I have heard of extremely lucky people who has done that before but that clearly isn't something that applies to everyone.

Yes, in my 15 years of options trading, I must say that I have never seen anyone make a string of 14 wins within one year or two without losing no matter what options strategy they use.

The good news is, you don't need to make 50% on every win nor do you need a string of 14 wins to make a million in options trading as long as you follow a sensible trading methodology and have lots of patience.

Making a million in options trading isn't about not losing. It's really about making more wins than losses. As long as you have a means of consistently making more wins than losses, you can make a million in anything as long as you have the patience to stick to the game. Yes, this is the same logic in any form of trading.

If it is the same in any form of trading, why then options trading?

The beauty of options trading is that it actually helps you achieve more wins than losses through 2 unique means; Convexity and Versatility.

Convexity means being able to potentially make more money than you can potentially lose. In futures trading or stock trading, you can potentially lose as much money as you can win. When the stock goes up by $10, you make $10 worth of profit and if the stock goes down by $10, you sustain $10 worth of loss.

There is no convexity. When you buy options, they will go up in value as long as the stock keep going in the correct direction (up for call options and down for put options) but if the stock goes the other direction, you will only lose as much as you used in buying the options, nothing more!

For instance, if you bought one contract of call options for a stock for $150 and the stock went up by $10, you call options would be worth $1000 but if the stock went down by $10, you would only lose that $150 that you used. That's convexity. As long as you use only money you can afford to lose or the maximum amount you are willing to lose on any single trade towards buying options, you will always have the advantage of convexity on your side.

Versatility is found in the vast array of options strategies that can be put together. Many options strategies allow you to profit not only when the underlying stock moves in one direction but in multiple directions!

Yes, in futures or stock trading, you only profit when the stock goes up or down (when you are short the stock or futures). However, in options trading, there are options strategies that allow you to profit when the stock goes up

OR down in both directions and options strategies that even allow you to profit from all 3 directions!

Yes, being able to profit in more than one direction greatly increases your possibility of winning and greatly enhances the possibility of consistently making more wins than losses!

So, can you become a millionaire trading options? Yes you can. In fact, from the properties of convexity and versatility mentioned above, options trading could actually make it easier for you to become a millionaire versus stock or futures trading. As such, the possibility is there and the odds are in your favor.

The final question to answer is, do YOU have what it takes to become a millionaire through options trading?

CHAPTER 5

Option Trading Advice

Those looking for option trading advice are usually either fairly new to the options market, or are experienced traders having some difficulty with their current trades and are hoping for an answer.

If you are among the first category you are probably looking for some advice about how to start options trading, what risks are involved and how to avoid them, how to trade safely and still make consistent profits.

If you are among the second category, there are ways to save or at least, salvage, losing trades, but this discussion must be left for other pages on this site.

So what is the best option trading advice for beginners?

The simple answer is, to make sure you first understand all there is to know about options trading, particularly the principle of time decay, before you risk any of your hard earned money.

Decide what kind of trader you wish to be. Do you want to be a day-trader, a short term trader or a longer term trader who only needs to check your positions to see if you need to adjust them once a day and has at least a monthly or longer strategy in place.

The next question you should ask is, what underlying financial instruments do you wish to connect your options to? Stocks, commodities or foreign currencies? Whichever one you choose, they each have their own set of characteristics.

Stocks can 'gap' overnight. Commodities can become very volatile. Currencies trade around the clock five days per week and are affected by economic news items.

Understand also, that the shorter timeframes you intend to trade, the higher the stress and if you hold your positions overnight, the greater risk of losing trades damaging out your account.

The Dangerous Way to Trade Options

In giving option trading advice, we would be remiss if we didn't bring to your attention the fact that, like any business, there is a high risk and a low risk way to do it.

If your intended strategy is to simply buy call or put options in an attempt to predict short term market direction and profit from these moves within a few days, you should understand that although this carries a potential high reward profile which makes it appealing, there is also a much greater risk that the price will go against you so that your losses can quickly outweigh your profits.

Many traders who try to predict short term market direction have cleaned out entire trading accounts.

You may believe you have found an option trading system that works for this type of strategy. But if you want some real option trading advice here, you should ask yourself whether you have the personal self discipline to take stop losses as well as stay in trades long enough to realize desired profits.

Do you have enough free time to be able to concentrate and act when the need arises? The high risk way of trading options often seems appealing to new traders due to the simplicity of its approach and the optimistic prospect of making big profits. But even well seasoned traders find market prediction difficult, so beware of systems that promise you the moon.

The Low Risk Way

Now here is the best option trading advice you may ever receive. If you understand the principle of time decay, you should learn how to use this to your advantage. It is far better to be on the selling side of an option contract than the buying side, due to this feature of options.

Taking positions with about a month or slightly more to expiry date and being on the selling side of option contracts puts you at a distinct advantage.

But you also want to add to this advantage, the art of adjustments. Even with the advantage of time decay on your side, the underlying price movement can come close to breaching your breakeven points before option expiry dates and this is where you need to know what to do.

If you adjust your positions correctly at this point, you not only save them from loss but guarantee further profits in the process.

In connection with the above strategy, you should consider trading indexes instead of individual stocks. The reason for this, is that you prefer a smooth price movement to a volatile one.

While a news item may unexpectedly the price of an individual stock it will not have much effect on the index to which that stock is related. An index is the aggregate of a group of stocks such as the Dow Jones, the Russell 2000, the OEX, QQQQ or the S&P500 in the USA. Options are available on all these indexes.

Trading double calendar spreads and iron condors on indexes and knowing how to adjust your positions when necessary, is one of the best trading methods I have found. My option trading advice to you is to at least familiarise yourself with these and allow yourself to trade with confidence.

Option Trading Terminologies: Must-Know

What about a little terminology on stock options trading? There are so many different terms that some are not familiar to those who do not trade. A few of the most common terms are below

Put- An option granting the owner the right to sell the security at a set price for a specific period of time

Call- An option granting the owner the right to BUY a security at a set price for a specific period of time

Bid- The price at which an options buyer is willing to buy an option or a stock

Ask- The price at which a seller is offering to sell an option or a stock.

At The Money- (ATM) A term that describes an option with an exercise price that is equal or close to the current market price of the underlying stock

Market Maker- An exchange member whose job it is to

Intrinsic value- he value of an option if it were to expire immediately with the underlying security at its current price; the amount which an option is in the money. If the option is out of the money it has no value and therefore no intrinsic value either

Time Value- The amount by which an option's total value exceeds its intrinsic value

Exercise- To invoke the right granted under the terms of a listed option contract. Call holders exercise to buy the underlying securities, while put holders exercise to sell the underlying securities

Delta- The amount by which an options price will change for a one-point change in the price of the underlying stock. Call options have a positive value and put options have a negative value

With a brief overview of the verbiage we can now discuss how to apply stock options in your trading arsenal.

There are options trading strategies to trade every kind of market that exits. From bull markets to bear markets and markets that are boring and flat, not going anywhere.

One of the most basic of option trading strategies, buying a call option is perhaps the easiest option trade. If you believe that a stock looks bullish or is going up you would want to use a call option to participate in the stocks run higher.

For example, if you thought that XYZ was going to be trading higher in a month from now you would buy a call. If XYZ was trading at $44.67 and you saw by looking at the charts that XYZ was just breaking out of a bull flag pennant and looked like it was going to $55 by the end of the month.

You could buy the at the money call at $45 for $1.20. Each option contract consists of 100 shares of stock. Therefore, if you buy 10 contracts you will be in control of 1000 shares of stock. This is why the leverage in options allows a person to control a large amount of stock for a fraction of the price.

You see if you bought 10 contracts at $1.20 that would cost you $1200. In order to buy 1000 shares of the actual XYZ stock it would cost you a whopping $45,000! This is why a regular person can get involved in stock options trading easier than actually buying the company's stock.

A put option would allow the buyer of the option to sell the underlying stock at a specified price. So if you thought that ABC was going to come crashing down because they are going to be sued by the SEC then you would buy the put option.

The same underlying principles apply to a put option the same as a call option contract. Just reverse the upside to a downside projection.

Surprisingly, only a small percentage of options are actually exercised. More expire worthless! That is right, most expire worthless!! The large majority of people sell the option contracts when they are up and have a profit before expiration. This is what majority of the professional traders do, as should you.

Exercising your option is a more difficult process that includes a few more steps that I will cover in the next article. Stock options trading techniques for the informed options trader.

Just like anything the more time you spend studying stock options trading the better you will become.

CHAPTER 6

Why Size Matters - Especially in Options Trading

In my previous eBook, "A Simple Guide to Investing in Turnaround Stocks - How to Successfully Invest in Stocks of Turnaround Companies" I mentioned the importance of financial analysis in stock market; "a good knowledge of analysis of stocks, and of market trends, is very necessary for anyone who desires to profit from the stock market. Stock analysis is really an art as much as a skill".

Investors can put themselves at a terrible disadvantage simply by sizing their positions incorrectly. This usually occurs when their position is too big relative to the risk and account size.

The key to getting the relative sizing correctly is understanding the risks associated with the position. Let me walk you through a likely trade scenario an investor not familiar with relative sizing might make.

For example, let's say on 7/31/14 an investor looking to take advantage of a short term move... sold call spreads in UVXY. UVXY is the PROSHARES Ultra VIX Short-Term Futures ETF. It attempts to replicate, net of expenses, twice the return of the S&P 500 VIX Short-Term Futures index for a single day.

On 7/31/14, UVXY was trading at $31.70. Let's assume on that day an option investor sold 20 $36/$39 call spreads (expiring 8/8/14)... collecting a premium of $0.57 or a total $1140 (minus fees and commissions).

Their goal is to get out of the position when the premium of the spread reaches $0.29... in which they would be buying back the spread for a profit of $560.

Taking profits at 50% of the premium collected is a great level to exit.

The max risk on this trade at expiration is $4,860.00 (the value of the spread minus the premium collected multiplied by the number of contracts times the multiplier).

$3 - $0.57= $2.43 x 20 = $48.60 x the multiplier of 100 shares = $4,860

However, the option investor is only willing to risk $1,000 on the position on a $50,000 portfolio. They will buy back the spread for a loss if it gets close to $1.05. On 7/31/14, the UVXY exploded... moving up more than 16% and closed at $31.70.

The investor felt that this was a good time to sell some premium as the UVXY has a history of sharp moves up followed by sharp declines.

Well, on 8/1/14, UVXY continued to climb higher as fears escalated both geopolitically and within the US equity market. It finished the day up nearly 10% and closed at $34.73. The value of the spread closed at $0.93.

Although the investor was looking at a paper loss of $720, they decided to get out of the position... if UVXY gapped up on the following Monday, it would probably get past the amount they were willing to lose.

(Note: UVXY is a product I wouldn't personally sell call spreads on... I'll explain my reason a little bit later.)

Now, when I typically short premium via structured trades... I size the trade to represent my max risk and play the odds. For example, if I were to put on this trade and was risking $1,000 on the trade... I'd sell 4 call spreads which would have a max risk of $972.

I'm not a proponent of stopping out of short premium trades.

As you know, most options expire worthless. However, there are cases where outliers occur and short premium trades go ITM and end up being losers.

By sizing my trades according to the amount I'm willing to lose... I'm not really stressed about any large overnight moves or morning gaps.

You see, I've already outlined my line in the sand.

In fact, this is one of the problems that I have noticed with those that use option strategies like iron condors.

Now, I'm extremely disciplined about following my rules. I know that if option volatility isn't elevated (or rich)... it doesn't make sense to add on more risk (to receive a greater premium) because that's how potentially big losses can occur.

Some of my clients achieve a great deal of success after a few weeks of learning my simple rules-based approach. However, when some tell me their profits, relative to their account size. I won't hesitate to let them know if they're taking on too much risk and sizing poorly.

Of course, some listen... but others will still size up to big... thinking that they will always have a chance to get out of position before it reaches max loss. But sometimes it doesn't work that way... stocks can gap up or down pre-market... and you may never get a chance to cut losses at desired levels.

If you're over-leveraged or sized incorrectly... one loss can wipe out several weeks or months of gains. Not only that, but if you're sized up too much... you might not have enough capital to adjust the position if it starts moving south.

I just wanted to mention my approach and what has worked for me... however, I understand that some investors like to use more leverage on their trades.

For that reason, I'll explain to you what else you need to take into consideration if you trade bigger than what you're willing to lose.

So where did our option investor go wrong?

First, they were trading options that were expiring in a little bit over a week. By selling 20 call spreads right off the bat, they didn't give themselves a whole lot of margin for error.

These short call spreads were still OTM, meaning the time decay and option volatility would really get sucked out of the option premium... if UVXY prices declined or even traded flat for a couple of days.

By fully sizing up, you leave yourself no margin for error.

In fact, if they still believed in the trade they would of have probably wanted to sell more call spreads at those strike prices or even further out for higher premiums.

However, they were forced to get defensive because they were sized up incorrectly.

(Note: The following Monday, UVXY traded at $31.50... down 9%... the value of the call spread was $0.47. On Tuesday, it rebounded to $35.93... the value of the call spread was back to around $1.00.

In 3 Ways To Keep More Profits & Know When To Sell, I explain the importance of closing out a position into strength.)

What other information can we use to figure out the right size if you're going to use more leverage?

Well, we need to know the risk associated with the trade or position.

Are there any event or headline risks?

Like an earnings announcement, conference call, analyst day, economic data release, Federal Reserve or other central bank meetings in the coming future, legal verdicts coming out, possible M&A or a reaction to earnings etc.

In this example, the UVXY ETF is associated with fear in the marketplace. The event or headline risk would be macroeconomic as well as geopolitical.

Are there any key technical levels?

Some questions to ask yourself: Is a key moving average that is broken, support or resistance levels violated, a spike below or above the VWAP or whatever technical indicator you're looking at.Now, I know some option investors who don't use price charts or technical analysis; some are very successful.

However, even if you don't... understand that there are other traders who do (with serious money behind them)... just knowing what levels they might be getting in and out of could be some useful information.

Is There Liquidity Risk?

During periods of high volatility... option and stock bid/ask spreads widen. Always play out a worse-case scenario in your head and try to calculate what the damage could be.

For example, the value of the spread when the investor got out was $0.93... but good luck getting out that price... most likely they would have had to pay up to exit the trade.

Sometimes the theoretical or mid-market price of an option... is just that... theoretical. The only thing that matters is what you can buy or sell at.

Are you giving yourself enough margin for error when looking at the volatility?

Over the last year, UVXY has had 23 (+/-) 10% single day moves or greater. In addition, option volatility can really take off in this ETF.

For example, on 7/24/14 the 30-day option volatility in UVXY was 105.3%... on 8/1/14 the 30-day option volatility was 158.63%... on 8/4/14 the 30-day option volatility went down to 132.1%... on 8/5/14 the 30-day option volatility was back to 152.1%

The 52 week high in option volatility in UVXY is 185.18%. Again, the investor in our example was probably thinking now is a good level to short some premium.

However, they wasted all there bullets without any room for error. Going all in or full size was not the right play in this situation.

You see, it's important to have some kind of perspective and understanding of the stock or ETF you're trading. The type of move we saw in UVXY is not uncommon relative to how it trades.

The option investor should have been aware of this and sized smaller.

Putting volatility levels into context is essential if you're going to be using options to express investment ideas.

Examine the time frame?

In my previous article , I share a story of one of my trades, where I had to close out a position because I was leaving to go to a dentist appointment.

I bought back some short puts for $0.10 expiring in an hour... those options that I bought back ended up closing deep ITM.

Again, near-term options have the potential from being deep OTM to deep ITM very quickly (and vice-versa). Position sizing is critical for near term options... it doesn't matter if you're buying or selling premium.

In many cases, if I do buy premium on an option expiring in a short time frame... I'll make it a binary trade.

Basically the premium spent on the position is what I'm willing to lose. For example, if options are $0.50 and I want to risk $500 max on the trade... I will buy 10 contracts. If I get my move... I'll take my profits.

Too many times... traders will buy 20 or 30 contracts under the same risk parameters... see the options go to $0.30 and get out... only to see the stock start moving in their direction... but no longer in the position.

The same could be said for those who sell weekly options on Thursday or Friday... the options have the potential to move very quickly... if you're sized up too much... you'll be out of the trade with a loss before you even got a chance to see the idea play out.

For longer term time frames you have to be more concerned about the volatility risk. A classic example is a biotech company that announces their drug results in a couple of weeks.

In anticipation, traders start buying and selling options in the contract month the announcement will be made. Of course, option volatility rises due to the uncertainty of the outcome.

Again, you almost have to treat these like binary trades as well. Even if you think you've got time on your options... anything could happen. For example, they could come out and say that will not have their results ready and change the announcement date to something else.

Those who bought option premium will see the value of those options lose a lot of value because of the volatility crush.

Putting it all Together

Relative sizing is one of the toughest things to get right as an investor or trader. If you invest for a long enough time... you're bound to get it wrong on some positions. The key is trying to get a deeper understanding of the risk associated with the position, what option factors influence (time, volatility, stock price movement) it and how.

For me, I like to play the number's game and let the probabilities work out... by sizing my positions with the max risk already set in place. However, I understand that some of you have a little bit more risk tolerance than me... so I wanted to show you what else to consider when taking on more risk by sizing up.

Obviously experience is the best teacher... but I'm also here to help.

In the UVXY example, the investor should have kept their sizing small in case they were off with the timing of the trade.

CHAPTER 7

Using Option Greeks in Option Trading

The option Greeks allow you to estimate how much an option contract should be worth as the price of the stock moves. Here are the three major ones and how to use them.

Trading stocks is easy, you already know how much you are going to make when you are right and how much you are going to lose when you are wrong. What is trick are options.

There are so many variables that go into pricing an option. So, how can you estimate how far an option will move if we are right? With the option Greeks, the delta, gamma, and theta.

So say we find a stock that is trading at $45 and we expect it to go to $50. We might want to buy the $45 option trading at $3, but we need some way to measure how much we can expect to make if we are right.

The first thing we can look at is the delta which will tell us how much an option will move for every 1 point move in the price of the stock. But the delta alone does not give us a good estimate. As the stock moves the Delta changes as well, so gamma tells us how much we can expect the delta to change for every 1 point move in the stock.

Let's say the delta for this option is $.50 and the gamma is $.10. Since we expect the stock to move $5 we would expect this option to increase $.50+$.60+$.70+$.80+$.90 or $3.5.

We would expect the option to be worth around $6.5 once everything is done. But that doesn't tell us the whole story. Options melt away as they get closer to expiration. To calculate how much they will melt away we can use theta. If theta is $.05 we would expect the option to lose $.05 for every 1 day we own it.

If we believe it will take around 10 days to make the move we can determine that the option will lose $.50 during that period, which means that we would expect the option to be worth $6 if it made the move that we were expecting it to.

CHAPTER 8

Options Trading Strategies - Commodity, Currency Spread and Carry Trading

Trading options can be highly profitable if done correctly. Options contracts get written on many different assets including currencies and commodities. One way is to spot trade these markets and the other way is to use options on these assets.

Several currencies and commodities such as gold and copper are intimately related. You can use this options trading strategy when you find the correlations between these currencies and commodities out of sync.

For example, South Africa is the world's largest exporter of gold. Its currency Rand is intimately correlated with gold prices in the international market.

When you find the spread between gold prices and RAND to be unusually wide and out of its historical relationship, you can simultaneously trade a gold call and a rand put in case the spread between RAND and gold prices is negative or the other way around.

Similarly, you can trade options if the spread between Australian Dollar and Gold prices widens and becomes out of sync with its historical relationship. You can also trade options when the spread between the Australian Dollar (AUD) and Reuters Commodity Index widens.

Reuters Commodity Index is a useful index that shows general commodity prices. What you are doing is betting on the fact that the spread is wider than the historical levels and is expected to narrow down to the normal.

Ever thought of carry trading. Many trader do it. You too can try it. Hedge funds are the expert in carry trading. One of their popular trading strategies is carry trading. You see no one wants the money to sit idle without making any return.

Carry trading is a nice way to profit with the interest rate spread between two currencies. You look for a currency pair that has one currency offering a much higher interest rate as compared to the other. You buy the high interest rate currency and sell the low interest rate currency.

Japanese Yen (JPY) was one of the most popular selling currencies for many carry traders in the last decade. Popular carry trading currency pairs is GBPJPY and NZDJPY. Another popular currency is selling Swiss Franc (CHF) and buying a higher interest rate currency.

The risk in carry trading is the potential of a large drawdown. Now, you can avoid the risk of these draw downs in carry trading by trading put and call options on these currencies.

One of the popular carry trading pair was GBPJPY. Many traders have encountered large draw downs by selling JPY and buying GBP. As a trader, you can reduce that risk by trading put and calls on these two currencies by using spread analysis on their historical correlations.

Traders tend to stay away from option trading because they just don't understand them. If you would like to become a better trader and make the most out of you investment dollar by limiting you risk, learning some of the options trading strategies can help you do just that. In this article we will take a look at the "bull call spread method" of trading options.

As with any trading "option" you will be paying a fee or a premium to have the right or "option" to call (buy) or put (sell) in 100 share lots for a specified amount of time at a negotiated price, anywhere from 21 days to over a year.

For instance: You may pay a $100 premium for the call option on GE at 35 ½ for 6 months and 10 days. (This is

OPTIONS TRADING

the most popular length of time because any profits made from that length are considered long-term capital gains and taxed at 25%)

Let's say GE's stock goes up and starts trading at 45 ½ before your option expires. You then exercise your option and realize a gain of $900. A gain of $10 a share, 100 shares =$1000-$100 premium = $900 net gain.

The bull call spread method favors a bull market, or an upward trend. This method will require you to buy a lower strike (price) call and writing a higher strike call at the same time.

The lower strike call has a better chance of being worth more because of the bullish trend in the market. You will write a higher short call to protect yourself from unfavorable swings in the market.

Example:

Long 1 September corn 350 call for 152
Short 1 September corn 400 call for 56

Days till expiration 33

Net premium 152-56=96 cents (9.5cents)

10(1 cent) in corn =$50

Net premium in $ value is 9.5 cents *$50/tick=$475

This is a great way to limit your risk and maximize profits. Hopefully you can realize the power of this sort of strategy and the unlimited potential of options trading.

As with any investment strategy, I recommend you first test this strategy with paper trades or a practice account to ensure you have a firm grasp on the theory behind the strategy before risking any real money.

Ask a trusted advisor if you have any question and be sure you know both the potential and the risks involved with any investment or trading strategy.

Option Trading Strategies For Long Term Investors

Option trading is typically associated with three different investor types. There are hedging strategies employed by large institutional investors, income-producing strategies for cash flow investors, and more aggressive trading strategies favored by speculators.

But where the does the long term investor fit in? Are there any option trading strategies that the conservative investor can employ to enhance his or her long term returns?

In fact, there are.

Leveraged Investing

There are actually a number of option trading strategies that can be employed by the long term investor. Leveraged Investing is the name I've given this approach, and these are the strategies I use myself.

The point of Leveraged Investing is to use options to acquire stock for a discount and then to generate additional returns above and beyond the actual performance of the stock itself.

Here are just two examples:

[Please note: in the interest of simplicity, commissions have been excluded from all examples.]

Example #1 - Writing Covered Calls. Writing covered calls is a popular, and generally conservative, income-producing strategy. A call option gives the holder the right, but not the obligation, to purchase 100 shares of the underlying stock at a certain price (strike price) by a certain date (expiration date).

Conversely, when you write, or sell, a call option on shares that you own, you sell (you receive a premium in the form of cash) someone else the right to purchase your stock at a certain price at or prior to the expiration date.

If you own 100 shares of a stock trading at $28/share, you could write a $30 covered call expiring in one month. If the stock closes above $30/share, you'll be obligated to sell your shares for $30/share.

But if the stock closes at or below $30/share, the call option will expire worthless and you're free to repeat the process. Either way, the premium received is yours to keep.

Writing covered calls is a great way to generate additional income from your investments, but the long term investor must take extra precautions to avoid being called out and forced to sell his or her long term holdings.

I call one such precaution, The 1/3 Covered Call Writing Strategy--it basically consists of writing covered calls on only a portion of your portfolio in order to give yourself greater flexibility and protection against sharp moves higher by the stock.

Example #2 - Writing Puts to Acquire Stock at a Discount. A put option, in contrast, gives the holder the right, but not the obligation, to sell 100 shares of the underlying stock at a certain price by a certain date. When you write, or sell, a put, you're essentially insuring someone else's shares against a drop below the agreed upon strike price.

Like writing covered calls, writing puts can be a great source of income. In fact, the risk-reward profiles for writing puts and writing covered calls are essentially the same.

Whereas call writers may write calls out of the money, at the money, or even in the money (the most conservative approach), put writers will typically write out of the money puts (e.g. writing a put with a $30 strike price on a stock currently trading at $32/share).

But for the long term investor, income is of less importance than the opportunity to buy a stock at a lower price that what it's currently trading at. Writing an at the money put will greatly improve the likelihood of acquiring the stock, and you'll also receive the most pure premium.

Example: Suppose you write an at the money put on a stock that you really like. If the stock is trading at $30/share and you write the put at the $30 strike price for, let's say, $2.50 in premium (or $250 in cash since each option contract represents 100 shares of the underlying stock) you're setting yourself up for a win-win situation. That's not to say you can't lose money on the deal, but look at the two possible scenarios.

If the stock closes at $30/share or higher, you keep the original premium you received (which, in our example, represents an approximate 8% return in one month). You're then free to write another at the money put for additional premium.

If the stock closes below $30/share, factoring in the premium you received, you end up purchasing the stock for $27.50/share. Obviously, if the stock gets cut in half, the premium you received will be small consolation, but what if the stock merely slips down to $29.50/share? You thought it was a good deal at $30/share and now you've acquired it for $2.50/share less.

As they say, options involve risk and may not be suitable for everyone. But not all option trading strategies have to be high risk propositions. Some approaches, in fact, may offer substantial benefits for the conservative investor. If you are a long term investor, it may be worth your while to conduct additional research to see if there should be a place in your portfolio for options.

Why Use Option Trading Strategies?

Many opportunity seekers are attracted to options trading as they have heard stories making promises of fast profits. The problem is that these traders come in thinking of nothing more than stuffing their bank accounts full of cash in a short period of time.

While this scenario is achievable the odds are certainly going well against you. In most cases achieving big profits in a short time period involves an extremely high risk options trading strategy.

The key to your success is finding a reliable strategy and mastering it. It is far better to pull off consistent gains rather than trying to hit a home run. Once you know one strategy, well you can learn others.

Below are some of the options trading strategies that you may consider.

Popular strategies to trade options include:

- Bullish on volatility
- Bearish on volatility
- Selling Credit Spreads
- Bearish strategies
- Selling Covered Calls
- Bullish strategies
- Neutral or non-directional strategies
- Calendar Straddle
- Strangles

The above list is in no way an exhaustive list, there are plenty of other strategies that you may employ. The purpose of this article is to just give you a small taste of some of the possibilities. Below I expand on a few.

Selling Credit Spreads - If you are looking for a strategy that does not involve marrying your stock options career, then this is one you could consider. There is nothing worse than following a strategy that requires you to monitor the market for every minute of the trading day.

You can complete what is involved with this strategy in around an hour a week and if done correctly you might be able to increase your portfolio by around 10-15 per cent monthly. They are great returns that really put to shame what the banks are offering.

To execute this strategy you need to know how to carry out a trend analysis on the market. Of course the scope of this article does not allow me to cover this further. You are best advised to join the mailing list on this site.

Bullish Strategy - If you are expecting the underlying stock of an option to increase then you could go with this strategy. The Bullish options trading strategies are brought into play when you as the trader expects the underlying stock price to increase in value.

You need to consider just how high the stock price is likely to go and within what time frame. The most likely strategy choice for a bullish trader is a simple call buying strategy.

This is quite popular with beginners. Other bullish strategies include Covered Straddle, Bull Calendar Spread and The Collar.

Complex Strategies - These include such things as iron condors, butterflies, straddles and strangles. Just where do they come up with the names used in strategies for options trading? Strange aren't they?

The ones I have listed here if followed correctly are generally low risk while at the same time being highly likely to be profitable. The disadvantage is that they are expensive, either due to the fact that you are trading expensive options or thanks to high brokerage fees which come about due to the number of trades involved.

You should remember that options are quite versatile trading instruments. With such great flexibility this is where many people get it wrong. They think that the more complicated an option trading strategy is the more successful it can be. In fact it can be quite the opposite.

The more complicated the strategy the more open you could be to risk while at the same time limiting profit potential.

As with any strategy you employ with your options trading business and treat it with respect. Don't trade live until you have given it a good test using a practice account. Only then should you consider running with it using your real money.

When learning how to trade options it is always advisable to only use risk capital when trading with real money. This means only use money that you can afford to lose if you have trades that go against you.

There you go that just touches the surface of options trading strategies. Of course you will want to learn more and then select a strategy to trade your options using a test account. From there who knows?

Always remember to not let things get out of hand. If you are learning a new strategy only trade with one contract at a time. If you go overboard you will soon find yourself out of control and headed towards disaster.

Options trading is not a race. You have time on your side and you should make the most of it. The market will still be here tomorrow.

The Best Option Trading Software

Option trading software was made to give day traders of all experience levels a leg up. It makes use of complex mathematical algorithms, it is able to detect and identify high probability trading ops in the market.

These algorithms compare contemporary market behavior to that of the past. From identifying overlaps between the two, you can learn everything about what to expect from that current stock in terms of subsequent behavior.

This is because stock behavior is extremely unique, so this technology builds huge databases of past market behavior, then applies that to real time behavior to find these overlaps 24 hours a day. With the entire analytical process handled for you, all you have to do is invest accordingly, armed with the knowledge of where and when to invest.

This means that casual investors can trade confidently on the same level as the pros who have done it for years.

It's also the most reliable way to invest because no emotions or other harmful pollutants are able to factor in and harm your trades.

With the success and popularity of this technology amongst traders of all experience levels and backgrounds, there are now more programs on the market than ever.

Looking for the option trading software? Consider this option trading software review for a look at the best of the best for realizing your financial independence.

Today, the best of the best is Best Penny Alerts.

One thing which makes Best Penny Alerts so effective is it only targets penny stocks. It's a completely different analytical process anticipating cheaper stock behavior, and the fact that this program only targets penny stocks it is much more effective than programs which go after all values of stocks.

It's so different anticipating the behavior of a cheaper stock because it takes far less influence to affect the price of a cheaper stock, so frequently you'll see penny stocks go on huge appreciations in the short term.

Take the first pick which I received from Best Penny Alerts as an example. I received the pick late Sunday night when it was valued at 15 cents. I placed an order for 1000 shares which seems like a lot but when you consider we're dealing with penny stocks it only cost me roughly $150.

That stock climbed to 19 cents in the first hour when the market opened the next morning. Over the course of that first day that stock steadily climbed, closing out at 31 cents.

The next morning I made a point to check in on that stock often. I was floored to find that it jumped 8 cents in the first hour, doubling how much it did in its first hour the day before which I attribute to the fact that outside investors noticed its previous day's appreciation.

About 5 hours in on that Tuesday, that stock reached its apex at 48 cents, just below the projection of 50 cents which I received from the program. This just goes to show the kind of profits which is out there when you know the exact moves to make in the market.

Sometimes, Best Penny Alerts delivers 4 or 5 consecutive trades so you can take a small amount of capital and turn it into 4 and 5 figures over the course of a few days, I really have never seen anything like it.

On top of everything else, Best Penny Alerts even comes with a money back guarantee in full. The publishers guarantee your satisfaction by offering you 60 day money back guarantee If you are dissatisfied with your results at any point in those 60 days, you can get your money back in full, no questions asked.

This enables you to test it risk free, receiving a handful of picks without risking a dime and gauging their performances in the real time market.

Even if you're fresh off the boat when it comes to stock investing or you don't have the time to devote to it, if you're ready to realize your financial independence I highly suggest you give the best option trading software a chance.

CHAPTER 9

Trading Options Like the Pros

In order to launch a successful career as a trader, you need to understand how to trade options. This is going to apply whether you're aiming to trade options for a living, become a day trader or even if you currently have a broker.

Understanding how to trade options will help you earn a profit with your investments, and eventually lead you to the kind of financial freedom that will allow you to live off your investments in comfort.

Naturally, this article can't be an exhaustive guide. In the same fashion that you wouldn't consider performing surgery after reading a quick guide on surgical techniques, you won't want to start trading unless you truly understand the fundamantals.

That being said, listed below are some of the important areas you'll need to take notice of in order to be able to trade options successfully.

1. Select the right exchange.

The Chicago Board Options Exchange is the largest and busiest options trading clearing house, but there are others around the world. Some specialize in niche product, such as commodities options or metals. Choose the exchange that is best suited to your trading background and your intended area of specialization.

2. Know your Terms.

Trading options, like any other professional craft, has its own special language. Before launching into trades, it is highly recommended that all novice traders get a hold of an index or glossary of trading terms, so that you don't have to learn them while trading.

While it may seem silly to read the trading equivalent of a dictionary, when you read that the stochastic are your Bermudan is looking good for the third date on the contract, you want to know what on earth you need to do.

3. Know your Emotions.

One of the little known secrets of how to trade options successfully is to get a firm grip on your emotions. The stakes are high when you're playing with your own money. How much can you really handle?

What will make you break down and make poor decisions? All experts will tell you that a trading system can only deliver strong results if the person governing it is following the system properly - and leaving emotion out of the equation.

If you become impulsive, you're not going to be able to manage your investments soundly.

4. Know your Limits and Stick to them.

Along with your emotions, knowing your own personal limits is important. What is the cap on your investments? What are your stop loss marks? What trades don't you know enough about to execute successfully?

The fundamental of how to trade options can be taught in books. However, the core areas of personal and professional knowledge that you need to succeed can only be discovered with reflection and objective examination of your skills, abilities, and comfort zone.

Don't load yourself up with technical tools if you don't understand them or if you are stressing yourself into an early grave. You may use options to create a like of financial prosperity and personal freedom, but before plunging in, educate yourself in all the key areas which will contribute to your success.

Conclusion

Stock options are investment vehicles that have recently become more popular, due to the wagering nature of our society. An option provides an individual with the right to purchase or sell shares of stock at a pre-determined price within a specified period. Most stock options traded on stock exchanges are American.

These American stock options may be exercised on any date between the day of purchase and the option expiration date.

One of the best ways for individuals to learn about the basics of this type of trading is to purchase a stock market guide. These guides are available in different formats and provide an overview of the world of options from a layman's perspective.

The best of the bunch start by providing basic definitions along with examples to illustrate their meaning. In later chapters, these cover various options trends and option trading strategies.

Knowledge is power in option trading, with this my eBook, I hope and wish you are now well equipped to join the train of option trading.

From the author's desk: Reviews are gold to authors! If you've enjoyed this eBook, would you consider rating it and reviewing it on amazon.com?

www.ingramcontent.com/pod-product-compliance
Lightning Source LLC
Chambersburg PA
CBHW021832170526
45157CB00007B/2778